W

S. [illegible]
PEOPLE

Published by RDO
6 Cotswold Business Village
Moreton-in-Marsh
Gloucestershire
GL56 0JQ
United Kingdom

© RDO 2001

A catalogue record for this book is available from the British Library.

Designed by
the workshop, Longhope,
Gloucestershire

Printed in China

ISBN: 1-903680-03-4

Show
me a
successful
business person

and I will
show you a
sales person.

*The fact is
we are all selling
one way or another.*

A really good sales person can only sell what they believe in.

Selling is a profession

&

it is the seller's responsibility to be a professional.

Think like a professional, speak like a professional, look like a professional, act like a professional *and you will be professional.*

A
NO
is only ever a
**NO
NOT
TODAY.**

THE SIX CYLINDERS OF THE PROFESSIONAL SALES PERSON.

Business Knowledge

Industry Knowledge

Company Knowledge

Product Knowledge

Selling Knowledge

Attitude

It's not what you know,
s who you know and it's what you do with who you know
that really matters.

The 6 P's-

*Proper
planning
prevents
particularly
poor
performance.*

*Don't ever
sell the product or service,
sell what it will do —*
**the results —
the benefits**.

Make it easy

for your customers

to do business

with you **NO VOICEMAIL**

FAST RESPONSE

MONEY BACK GUARANTEE

BEFORE EVER
ATTEMPTING TO SELL
A PRODUCT OR SERVICE,
YOU MUST FIRSTLY
SELL YOURSELF
BY BEING
GENUINELY INTERESTED
IN YOUR CUSTOMER.

YOU CAN MAKE
MORE FRIENDS IN
TWO MONTHS BY
BECOMING INTERESTED
IN PEOPLE THAN YOU
CAN IN TWO YEARS
BY TRYING TO GET
THE OTHER PERSON
INTERESTED IN YOU.

To become an interesting person all one has to do is be interested in others.

The greatest secret
to successful selling
is to ask the right questions -
**ask the right question and
you get the right answer.**

Ask more, tell less.

THE WORST THING
ABOUT A BORE
IS NOT THAT HE WON'T
STOP TALKING
BUT THAT HE WON'T
LET YOU STOP
LISTENING.

We have two ears and one mouth and that's the way they should be used.

DON'T JUST DO WHAT YOUR CUSTOMERS WANT,

plan ahead and create what they didn't know they wanted

AN EXECUTIVE SALES PERSON IS A MIND-MAKER UPPER.

The fear of loss
is a bigger buying motivator
than the opportunity
of gain.

BEING MISERABLE IS A HABIT,

BEING HAPPY IS A HABIT

*and
the
choice
is yours.*

Whether you believe you can *or* believe you can't,

you're absolutely right!

Don't ever over-promise and under-deliver,

how about under-promising and over-delivering?

It is really rather stupid if you do the same thing next year as you have done this year and hope for a different result.

It is not the
employer
who pays the wages:
employers only
launder
the money.

It is the customers who pay the wages.

LUCK

is what happens when preparation meets opportunity.

A lie
may take care
of the present,
but it has no future.

Opportunities multiply when they are seeds, but die when they are neglected.

Fear less hope more, eat less chew more, whine less breathe more, talk less say more, hate less love more *and all good things are yours.*

A guaranteed way of conquering fear is to do the thing you're afraid to do.

Yesterday is *experience*,
tomorrow is *hope*,
today is for getting
from one to the other
as best one can.

THE WILL TO WIN

IS NOT NEARLY AS

IMPORTANT AS THE WILL

TO <u>PREPARE</u> TO WIN.

**Those who can't
laugh at themselves
leave the job
to others.**

The *only* place you find success before work is in the dictionary.

**A
true
friend**
is someone who is there for you
when he would rather be
anywhere else.

The more you STRETCH the truth, the easier it is to see through it.

A study of economics usually reveals that the best time to buy anything is **last year**.

DIGNITY IS THE
CAPACITY TO HOLD
BACK ON THE TONGUE
WHAT NEVER
SHOULD HAVE BEEN ON
THE MIND IN THE
FIRST PLACE.

Brilliant diplomacy is thinking twice before saying nothing.

He who laughs first doesn't always laugh last.

Any problem you can solve with a cheque isn't a problem, it's an expense.

People who wait
for all conditions
to be perfect
before acting

NEVER ACT.

HAVE YOU EVER NOTICED HOW THE EMPTY CAN MAKES THE MOST NOISE?

*If you're not happy
with what you've got now,
what makes you think
you'll be happier
with* **MORE**?

*Dumb sales people
tend to become
best friends with other
dumb sales people.*

If you don't ask you don't get.

IN BUSINESS AS IN LIFE,
YOUR CHANCES OF BEING
RUN OVER ARE DOUBLE
IF YOU STAY IN THE
MIDDLE OF
THE ROAD.

If you're skating on thin ice, skate really fast.

You'll never get *ahead* of *anyone* as long as you try to get *even* with them.

BUSINESS
IS LIKE
RIDING
A BICYCLE,

EITHER
KEEP
GOING
FORWARD
OR YOU'LL
FALL
OVER.

HAVING
something
to say
s always more important
than
WANTING
to say something.

Sometimes when a person with money meets a person with experience, the person with experience ends up with the money and the person with the money ends up with the experience.

MORE PEOPLE

GET INTO TROUBLE

FOR THE THINGS

THEY <u>SAY</u>

RATHER THAN

FOR THE THINGS

THEY <u>DO</u>.

The best time to save money is when you have some.

Don't be afraid to say,
I DON'T KNOW -
*people will respect you much more
and will always place more weight
on what you say, because they know
you are right.*

Worrying about what is right is always more important than worrying about who is right.

How about doing
today
what you don't want to do
or you might be tempted
to put it off until
tomorrow
or
another day.

Are you *passionate*
about what you do?
Are you grateful you can do it,
are you hopeful and expectant about
what the future might bring?

IF WE DID ALL THE THINGS WE ARE CAPABLE OF WE WOULD LITERALLY ASTOUND OURSELVES.

A PERSON WHO IS SURE
NOTHING CAN BE DONE
IS USUALLY THE PERSON
WHO HAS NEVER DONE
ANYTHING

Change your *thoughts* and you will change your *attitude.*

FAILURE IS NOT IN FAILING, IT'S IN NOT TRYING.

WHY NOT GO OUT ON A LIMB– THAT'S WHERE ALL THE FRUIT IS.

A good
marriage is a
PRIZE,
you do not
get it for
nothing.

Money will buy
all kinds of things
for your family
BUT
*it won't buy
their love.*

discipline IS A HABIT OF TAKING CONSISTENT ACTION UNTIL ONE CAN PERFORM WITH UNCONSCIOUS COMPETENCE.

Integrity *gives you
real freedom
because you have nothing
to fear
since you have nothing
to hide.*

It was **character**
that got us out of bed,
commitment that moved us
into action
and **discipline** that enabled us
to follow through.

You build a successful career regardless of your field of endeavour by the dozens of little things you do on and off the job.

SUCCESS

is the sum of small efforts
repeated day *in* and day *out*.

It's amazing what happens when you recognise your good qualities, accept responsibility for your future and take positive action to make that future even brighter.

You are the way you
are because that's the
way you want to be,
if you really wanted
to be any different
you would be in the
process of *changing*
right now.

not **what** happens to you
ut **how** you handle what happens
at makes *the difference*.

When you choose to be **pleasant** and **positive** in the way you treat others, you have *also* chosen in most cases how you are going to be treated by others.

LAUGHTER

**is good for business;
it can reduce stress,
enliven meetings
and spur creativity.**

There has never been
an undisciplined person
who was a champion
in every field
of human endeavour -

*temporary pain,
lifetime gain.*

A commitment

is doing what you said you would do long after the feeling you said it in had passed.

One example of
good manners
is to be able to
put up pleasantly
with those
who demonstrate
bad manners.

It takes less
to keep an
old customer satisfied
than to get
a new customer
interested.

YOU MAY HAVE
A DISABILITY
BUT YOU DON'T HAVE TO
BE DISABLED,
BEING DISABLED
CAN BE A STATE OF MIND.

If at first you don't succeed,

sky diving is not recommended for you!

A great negotiation tip,

value for money,

quality,

service –

say to your prospect,

which one would you

like to leave out?

LIFE doesn't always work the way we would like it. Some people keep complaining and whining about the way things should be but never will be.

Once we begin to accept responsibility for ourselves, we can be on the way to happiness.

If you're too busy to relax,

YOU'RE TOO BUSY.

Nobody can do **everything**
but everybody can do **something**
and if everybody does something
everything will get done.

It's worth considering
that winners can be like
TEABAGS,
you never see their true strength
until they are in hot water.

PASSION

**IS A FANTASTIC WORD,
IT IS IRRESISTIBLE,
IT IS SO POWERFUL,
IT IS ALSO SO PERSUASIVE.**

The expression
'you can lead
a horse to water
but you can't
make him drink'
is of course true.
**In selling the seller
knows the job
is to make the
horse thirsty.**

A GREAT CUSTOMER CARE TIP

Life is like a game of tennis;

the player who serves well seldom loses.

Success can be so simple,
so why complicate it?

Firstly, work out exactly
what you want to do

and secondly,
go ahead and do it.

KEEP AN OPEN MIND, DISCUSS BUT DON'T ARGUE – IT'S A MARK OF A SUPERIOR MIND TO BE ABLE TO DISAGREE WITHOUT BEING DISAGREEABLE.

Make
promises
sparingly
and
keep them
faithfully
no matter what it costs.

REMEMBER THAT A PERSON'S NAME IS TO THAT PERSON THE SWEETEST & MOST IMPORTANT SOUND IN ANY LANGUAGE.

It takes a
BIG
thinking brain
to admit
when one
makes a mistake
or one is wrong.

Small brains
can't cope.

A SMILE
HAPPENS IN A FLASH
AND THE MEMORY
OF IT SOMETIMES
LASTS F O R E V E R.

None are so **rich** that they can get along without a smile and none so **poor** that they are richer for its benefits.

The three C's that do so much harm, destroy so many relationships and rarely achieve anything -

Criticising, Condemning & Complaining.

We very rarely regret
the things we have
DONE,
we are more
likely to regret
the things we
HAVEN'T DONE.

You can't
build a reputation
on what you are
going to do

but on what you do do

If you're not convinced you *can't* convince.

VERY FEW PEOPLE BUY PRICE, THEY BUY VALUE AND PERCEIVED VALUE TO THEM.

It is better to be silent
and thought a fool
than to speak
and remove all doubt.

To achieve successful sales results, think before you act and act fast after you have thought.

BEFORE
PICKING UP THE PHONE
DECIDE EXACTLY

WHAT YOU WANT
TO ACHIEVE FROM THE
PHONE CALL.

The professional sales person's most used words –

What,
Why,
When,
How,
Where,
Who.

PAST CUSTOMERS CAN BE THE BEST SOURCE OF NEW BUSINESS.

*Never forget
a customer,
never let
a customer
forget you.*

Customers buy

more by their

eyes

than they ever do

by their ears.

The most important word in selling is Why -

"do you mind me asking you why"

Courage

is not the absence of fear,

it is the **conquest** of it.

Better words

Don't say change,	say **improve** or **develo**
Don't say pay,	say **own** or **invest**
Don't say sign,	say **agree** or **authorise**
Don't say when I sell,	say **when you own**

People don't buy your products, services or ideas, they buy how they imagine using them will make them feel.

When I want to remember how to sell, I simply recall how I like to buy.

PEOPLE HATE TO BE SOLD BUT THEY LOVE TO BUY.

It's more fun
and more
financially successful
when you stop trying
to get what you want
and start helping
other people
get what they want.

ONE OF
THE GREAT PLEASURES
IN LIFE
IS DOING
WHAT PEOPLE
SAY YOU CANNOT DO.

Don't just
do what
your customers want,
plan ahead
and create
what they didn't know
they wanted.

EXPERIENCE IS THE HARDEST KIND OF TEACHER, IT GIVES YOU THE TEST FIRST AND THE LESSON AFTERWARDS.

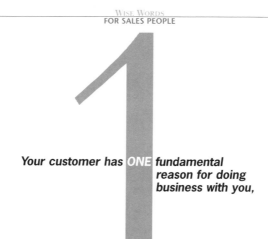

Your customer has ONE fundamental reason for doing business with you,

so that he himself can do MORE business.